Lisa's Flying Electric Piano

POEMS

by Kevin Rabas

March 2009

Editor: Dennis Etzel, Jr.

Woodley Press
Department of English
Washburn University
1700 SW College Avenue
Topeka, KS 66621

Printed by Lightning Source

ISBN-10: 0-9817334-0-9
ISBN-13: 978-0-9817334-0-1

Library of Congress Control Number: 2009921457

Cover photograph: "KC Alley" by Dave Leiker
Cover piano keys drawing by Ashton Ludden

Cover design: Eric Sonnakolb

Back cover author photo: Max McCoy

Text design and layout: Pam LeRow

To contact the author, write to:
Kevin Rabas
PO Box 274
Emporia, KS 66801
krabas@emporia.edu

Acknowledgements:

The author gratefully acknowledges the editors of the following publications, in which versions of the following poems first appeared:

"Playing Muddy Waters…" and "Fall Up" in *Eclipse*

"Between Rains" in *Pinyon*

"Ballet Slippers" and "Driving into Autumn" in *The Mid-America Poetry Review*

"Hearing, Watching Claude…" in *The Quill*

"Summer Rain for Melvin" and "After Stephen Hawking's…" in *I-70 Review*

"Oedipa Discovers the Circuitry of Real Estate: A Montage on Pynchon's *The Crying of Lot 49*" and "That One-Legged Man" in *Coal City Review*

"In Jonathan's Office" in *The Midwest Quarterly*

"Lisa's Flying Electric Piano" and "You'll Need Them All One Day*"* in *seveneightfive*

"Slow Words" and "Economics of Summer Rain" in *The Louisiana Review*

"Cruisers" in *Touchstone*

Words of Thanks:

I would like to thank my family for their continuing support, including (but not limited to) Lisa, Eliot, Joyce, Gary, and Alicia. I would like to thank Dennis Etzel, Jr., my editor and friend, and I also would like to thank all of the kind folks at Woodley Press for helping make this poetry manuscript a book.

Thanks also go to family and friends who saw this manuscript in earlier versions and offered advice and affirmation, including Ruth Moritz, Jonathan Holden, Allison Rose Lopez, Lisa Moritz, Joyce Rabas, Matt Porubsky, Greg Field, Doug Talley, Paula Prisacaru, and Phil Hull.

A special thank you goes to Dan Jaffe for his editorial advice and guidance.

Thanks to my visual artists, as well: Dave Leiker, Ashton Ludden, and Eric Sonnakolb.

Thank you to Erin Minneman for CIP layout and design work, and thank you to Pam LeRow for final layout and design work.

I would also like to thank Emporia State University. Part of this manuscript was written during the time I was on an Emporia State University Research and Creativity Grant.

Contents:

Introduction:

I feel fortunate and honored to introduce these poems by my friend Kevin Rabas almost as much as I am honored to call him a friend. You will find this second book of his to follow the same melodic journey as his first book, maybe with more of a resonance. His voice has travelled miles to get here. His poems are the evidence.

Indeed, these lyrical poems fit the definition of the lyric— where the musical meets the personal. If you've ever caught one of Kevin's jam sessions or performances, you might catch the rhythms that find their ways into this book. You will meet the people he has met, be in the rooms where he has played, join in the jam:

> Samson plays piano
> with one hand, and with the other,
> and with his mouth, he plays trumpet,
> "Volare," while Dave sings his best
> Sinatra impersonation. It is going to be
> one of those nights.

There are wonderful people in these words. The tone Kevin sets allows us *to be* in the poem, another function of poetry:

> Play that way now
> every time, as if what you rumble
> across the drums is a language,
> and what you are asking for now is love.

We share in his love for music and language.

You can find a spirituality in this work, "the birth of religion," get lost in the impressions streets can make, tangled in what love is or can be. These are neighborhoods of the mind, and some of them are not pleasant. I am thankful that Kevin shares in his experiences, far from the confessional mode that would drop a bomb into the reader's lap before running away. These poems of survival show a poet who has survived wiser, braver in the telling without the woe-is-me our culture can be submerged in.

You will also find the circle of family, going from the speaker's childhood to the speaker's son. And of course, there is Lisa,

Kevin's wife. She is also a musician, and you will find her here
with her Flying Electric Piano:

> …I dreamt, at last,
> of turning corners slow, and of a keyboard
> rising in flight and floating across town,
> playing a well-known sonata as it flew.

After reading Kevin's poems, I can still see her Flying Electric
Piano soaring above our heads, making loops and dazzling us. It
is Kevin's poems that make this happen.
   The last line of "In Jonathan Holden's Office" describes how
Holden places a poem to the trashcan:

> Jonathan motioned to the trashcan, and his hands
> brought a poem to its green lip, as if saying,
> "This is what you must do sometimes."

Maybe so, Jonathan, but not in the case of this work. Pour a
drink, put on some Jazz, sit back with this book and enjoy!

Thank you, Kevin!

Dennis Etzel Jr.
February 2009

1. Slow Words

Slow Words

The mailbox is now empty.
Your letter has not arrived.
I check my email about 10 times a day.
There is a problem with how fast we can learn
the news of each other's lives,
and I would rather take the slow train instead
of the fast plane overhead. I order two books
over the internet in 45 seconds, when I could have
shopped all day at the used bookstore in the next,
bigger town and read so long and come away
with nothing in my hands, walking over the wood threshold
and out into the 100 degree sun. All week
the sun is slated to bake us. Meteorologists all agree
it won't let up until the weekend rain comes,
when I will most likely open the black metal lid
to our porch mailbox and find inside your reply,
and, for me, it may mean a day spent inside
listening for the pulse of your words on the page,
watching your blue pen loops for signs
of your voice, your mouth, your words.

In Jonathan's Office

for Jonathan Holden

On Jonathan's office wall, a chalkboard
with a big egg drawn. He motioned,
and I sat down among the stacks
of papers and books. One fan gust
and the room would lift
like a flock of pigeons. Jonathan
asked me if I spoke German,
and I said I had been to Erfurt
and Leipzig. I knew a phrase or two.
He spoke to me in quick sentences,
paragraphs of the language. At first,
I struggled to keep up, but later
I surrendered to the waves of German
coming in shutters through his bearded
lips. It was poetry to me, whatever it was he said,
and I knew then I was in an office of genius.
Jonathan motioned to the trashcan, and his hands
brought a poem to its green lip, as if saying,
"This is what you must do sometimes."

Fall Up

Gunkle and I had this big mirror between us, hefting it
into the back of his blue pickup truck. Gunkle's part retarded,
a giant in blue jeans and green Crocs, wearing a white T-shirt
with battery acid on it. His glasses are thicker than my thumb.

So, we grab hold of this monster mirror, and it glints,
and we both look into that mirror, noticing the clarity
of that blue sky and those green sycamore leaves reflected
so perfectly that is appears you could just dive on into that mirror
and sink into the sky, and we think the same thing.
"You could fall up," Gunkle says, "and just keep on falling.
Nothing would stop you." And that was the way of it.
Gunkle's mind was now my mind, and I was in that mirror
falling on up through those white smoke clouds
headed towards an orange sun.

Gunkle and I stacked box bed springs on top of that mirror,
and some branches from out front, and I could hear that large
    mirror crack,
but I think Gunkle and I could still see it—
that vision of sinking into sky, drowning
with only the sun to hold us up.

Spare Change

It happened on the sidewalk in San Francisco
about a block from the library. I had stopped
on the sidewalk to take a look at a homeless woman.
She was asleep behind a grocery cart full of
clothes and bulging tan and blue plastic bags.
Beneath the cart's crisscrossed wires were coins,
mainly nickels and pennies. Coins, I take it,
that had fallen through her cart. A man in a dark
business suit, carrying a briefcase, stooped
and picked up a handful of coins, then walked
away, his black, shined shoes carrying him
to his desk, I assumed, on a high floor
somewhere above us, the coins
jingling in his pocket when he walked.
Change taken. Change used.
Change easily forgot.

Driving into Autumn

You drive with your windows open
through the dark at the beginning
of autumn, the leaves not yet dropped
to the ground, but held,
bright and burning, at the tips
of the tree limbs, as one might hold
a lit match a moment longer
before puffing it out.

Cruisers

Anna kept saying she wanted to drive.
I let no one drive my car, but I drove them
through the streets of Mission, a cop
car tailing us for miles, a man in a black hat
in our rearview mirror, tailing us by 30 feet,
15 feet, enforcing something, keeping pace.

Matt took off his ball cap, and Anna
let her long blonde hair flow, the air
vents in the sides of the car whistling,
vents that looked like gills on trout,
gills for allowing us to move through
the streets as if they were streams.

He tailed us for more than 12 blocks.
When he turned onto a side street,
we reached out our arms into
the air moving around us in waves,
and we felt like we were stealing something.

Summer Rain and Melvin

Out of the coffee shop window the umbrellas went
up, and crowds fled under the cover
of great green awnings, a moment
when the music stops.
I spot Professor Melvin Landsberg
without his new four-pronged cane, moving
between the big grey drops,
walking beyond the reach of his vertigo,
cured and fleet, another
figure with a thin coat on,
scrambling to the base
of brick buildings, looking
deep into the yellow windows
of the shops, then pushing past
folks on the sidewalk,
taking to the street and moving beyond
the common shopgoer's line of sight,
until, like the first streetlight lamp
or an early evening star, he is a small spot
on the night horizon.

2. Head Injury Blues

for Jodie, who would not eat

When it comes time for circle,
we are asked what we are proud about,
and the thin girl says, "I haven't
pulled down my pants for a man
in over two weeks." And we clap.
And she puts her chin up, and she
puts her chin back down and looks at her lap.
I think I am beginning to like her.
She has dark hair that flows around
her shoulders as I imagine
Joan Baez's hair would. Thin girl
is about 18, and she refuses to eat.
At breakfast, we pull trays from a metal
shelving unit that has wheels. I take eggs,
and she takes eggs. I sit across from her.
She says her name is "Jodie," and I say, "Kevin."
I say, "Eat," putting my fork underneath
the Day-Glo yellow scrambled eggs and lifting
a batch to my lips. "It's good. Please," I say.
And she does, and we match forkful for forkful
for a while, across the table, and I think that
if I die now, I will have done one good thing.
Her toe touches mine beneath the table,
but then the dogs come. It is pet time. My wife arrives,
and Jodie leaves just as she sees my wife. I pick a Blue Heeler,
and I pet it. I smile at my wife. I hug her. I kiss her.
I realize, by her expression, by how she holds her body,
that my wife wants me here. Kept here.

Bent Credit Cards

I had our last credit card in my hands,
and I bent it until it came apart.
I gave you half. You said, "Let's forget
about all of this and go out
dancing." Tonight we were deciding
to divorce. This would be the last
time we spoke out of court.
Afterward, the art that you made,
our photos, and the art that our friends
had given us would all go. We would
not talk. Between us a silence
would settle. I would see
you in traffic, near the holidays,
and in that cold you hung your head
out the side window of a friend's
hunter green SUV, and said,
"Merry Christmas, Kevin." And I pulled over
to cry. There was that buoyancy and joy
still in your voice during that last time
that I saw you, when I was returning
from my new love's apartment, her kisses
still wet upon my lips.

Waterdeep

My wife, J, said she thought she saw flames
coming from their heads. "The spirit
was with them," she said. I was not sure
I could believe. But I loved and believed
in her passion, and it was a conversion
for me to look up at the stage and think,
This is what I know. This is what
I would say and do, if I were playing again.
I met my wife after a gig. She helped me
carry my drums into my blue Blazer,
and I was in love with this woman
who thought to help, who was a fan,
who did not mind carrying cymbal stands
across the frozen parking lot, stepping
through the snow. At night, weeks later,
she said she saw a dark spirit at the edge
of my bed, by the bed post, waiting.
Again, I did not believe, but I tried
to comfort her. In time, she would leave
me in a mental institution. I swung
a gray scarf she bought me around my neck,
and I left, as I came, of my own will,
filled out the papers, and we were through.
Divorce came. Divorce went. She said,
"Take care of yourself," after the divorce trial,
and I said I would. Listening to the band
we spent time loving, Waterdeep, I listen
for the cracklings, and the silence between us
grows cold. J said, when she left,
"Let's never speak again," but I listen
for her voice, and in crowds
and on sidewalks, I once watched for her.
There are no words between us,
only this music. So, I set the CD spinning,
and when I listen closely, somewhere
beneath the voices I think I hear flames.

Think of the Sun

Prisoners write no stories. Norman
Mailer said it right. But some
of us do. It is an act,
like a near drowning, going
back into the black ocean,
seeing it all happen again,
but this time at high tide
at night. We do it, if we can.
We do it because we can,
and because perhaps it is
the only way to know,
Yes, now, it was real,
and, yes, now, we know,
it is past. We dream now only
of the sun. It is our God.
The night is only a nightmare
and a death, a place the past
may rise in, like a black-hawk
that can enfold sparks
of daylight in its dark wings.
Sometimes it seems
none of us will die.

Goodbye: A Head Injury Poem

My ex-wife leaned out the window
of the hunter green SUV, and said,
"Merry Christmas, Kevin," and I knew
it was over. I pulled to the side
and let traffic pass. I thought back
to how it all had ended, starting
with a pick up basketball game,
my head hitting the blonde wood
of the floor; the pills I took that evening
(2 Advils, a multivitamin, a calcium pill,
and a B vitamin, for strength):
how I knew something was wrong,
but the pills didn't fix it; how the others
at the dinner party went to the other room,
asking what was wrong. My face had lost
all emotion. I was a zombie to them.
It is quite common, I read later, for the emotions
to drain from the face, when the head is injured.
You become blank, and others wonder why.
The emotions returned, though. As I sat
in my car at the edge of the road, I thought,
"They all came back too late." And her car,
It kept going, and I thought about how,
when I was healing, she would sing
to me at night, psalms, and how
I dragged our bed across the room,
so I could only hear her.

How It Happened

I was knocked down
in a pick up basketball game.
The doctors said my brain bounced
against my skull, causing bleeding
of the brain. I jumped back up,
with a mild concussion and contusion,
and I played out the game, missing shots,
covering my man. Afterward, I tied
a gray scarf around my eyes,
in the combat room, and I meditated.
I sat cross-legged. I waited, and peace came
to me, and I drove home across snow
to our apartment in Manhattan, Kansas.
But something had changed. Like a spark set
in a pile of rags, my emotions came now
in flames, and I used my mind to douse them.
Anger came. Fear came. The world, for me,
spun much faster. Going to the grocery store
was like walking into combat. Everything
assaulted me: the lights, the overheard conversations,
the movement, the aisles of brightly covered boxes
and cans. My senses overloaded, I would go home
and sleep, for hours, in the middle of the day,
healing. My wife left me. She took most everything
in the house. I did heal, slowly. I wrote long-hand
to remember. I went to Yellowstone, and I climbed
the hills and mountains. I fished for trout. I lived
in my sister's trailer, and I watched the snows melt.

3. Playing for Dave

Jack McCann's Own Hometown Marching Band

"Attack the drum," Jack McCann said.
"If you make a mistake,
I want to hear it. I want everyone
to hear it. So, make it loud.
Be proud of that mistake,
then fix it later. Let's hear
you now, every note."

Jack wore a white cowboy hat
and had some silver teeth.
He'd been in the military,
and had us play the songs
of each branch of the service.
My favorite was "Anchors Aweigh."

We were kids, 10-15 years old. At first, we didn't
have equipment. We held a snare drum
with one hand and hit it with the other
with a stick. We were a hometown
marching band. That first night,
Jack marched us in circles:
drummers, clarinets, flutes, saxes, trombones.
I thought he might just be
the true Music Man,
our own Harold Hill. I had seen
that musical, and I believed.

Solo for Timpani

for Kara

Tighten the timpani
until the sides go copper.
With two soft cartwheel mallets,
boil the low drumhead
until only elephants can hear.
Play that way now
every time, as if what you rumble
across the drums is a language,
and what you are asking for is love.

Playing for Dave

At the bar, his back to us, a man
slaps his bald head over and over
with his hands. Samson plays piano
with one hand, and with the other,
and with his mouth, he plays trumpet,
"Volare," while Dave sings his best
Sinatra impersonation. It is going to be
one of those nights. When the set
is over, one of Dave's ladies
asks me out into the parking lot,
where she teaches me
to shotgun a beer. I am 19
going on 20, and beer sprays
between her breasts, and she
laughs. I try now, and it is like
breathing beer, like snorkeling
in an ocean of it, and coming up
and forgetting to blow out hard,
spouting. When we return,
through the western-style wooden
swing doors, Samson is already
on piano again, his trumpet wrapped
in a blue towel on top. Dave is singing
"Caravan," and I am expected to solo,
which is what I do best. But my ankles
are rubber. So I use only my sticks,
my feet fading into the carpet,
the bass drum pedal, quiet, silent,
waiting for my foot to come down.
I swim through the set, my sticks drawing
circles, triangles, and squares across
the cymbals and the drums, and I look
for Dave's girl, but now
she is gone, and where she sat
there is Dave's wooden rabbit-head cane,
situated like a Rasta's staff, marking
the place she had been.

Hearing, Watching Claude "Fiddler" Williams at The Epicurean in KC

1.
Dave wore an all
white suit, when we sat in
at The Epicurean,
a dim-lit club, where
black intellectuals played chess
in the half-light, and 85-year-old Fiddler
sang, pulling on his red suspender straps,
and then, in a moment of private beauty,
did soft shoe up front,
in the sand on the floor.

2.
Dave hammed it up,
singing first like Sinatra
and then like Louie,
and when we broke,
Dan Mills in his characteristic
captain's hat said, "You
remind me of that nice young man
with the blond curls, only you
don't play sax."
"Kenny G?"
"Yes, Kenny G. Will you help me
to the bathroom. I don't get around
much anymore." So, I lent him
my shoulder, and he leaned on me
as he pissed. His wife said,
"Go up there and play again."
Dave said, "Presenting the best
young drummer in KC…"—
(how could I live up to this)—
and I played it as hot as I could,
comping behind Tim Blair,
just off a cruise ship, full
of melody and fire, chops
and control, ready now

to play the phrases
he had withheld on that
slow moving boat.

Claude watched us
from the side of the stage,
his fiddle and bow resting
against his leg. When Tim finished,
Claude led us all to the top
of the tune. The melody
was his to finish.

Claude pulled the bow
across his fiddle strings,
quick and lithe,
spelling out the melody
to "Lester Leaps in"—
Fiddler, who played guitar
for the KC Basie band—
Fiddler, who grunted
to mark a rest—
Fiddler, who held the stage
like a magician holds a dove in his hands
—Fiddler, who keeps up
with the younger players on the stand,
then pulls up and flies right past.

You Should Tune

At that gig, Doug refused to tune.
We were in the coffee shop
at Barnes & Noble, and Doug said,
"I am beyond tuning." I laughed, and said,
"Don't we tune because we care?"
"I don't care anymore," he said. And Matt,
on bass, said, "Man, you really do
need to tune." And Doug said, "Forget it."
And I said, "Tune, man. You need to tune,
or I'm leaving." And Doug said, "Go. Leave."
And I did, picking up my hihat and snare drum
as I left. I didn't play a note that night.
I hummed one of Doug's tunes
as I walked the sidewalk into the parking lot
to my car.

A month before, in the studio,
Doug wasted an hour of our money
trying to tune his guitar. And now,
and now he would not tune.

Matt promised me he would kick
Doug's ass when we saw him again.

Singing Muddy Waters at the Emporia Art Walk:
A Birthday Poem for Gary Holcomb

The sun is out in full today
for the first time in weeks,
radiating in hot wisps of grey on grey,
and we are on the sidewalk
outside Flint Hills Music,
our bassist behind the counter,
working the crowd.
So, it is just you and me.
Your blond guitar shines
against the sun, and my metal brushes
go hot in my hands. You wear
a straw Kangol hat and a black
T-shirt that says The Clash.
Next to us, under a sun tent,
Girl Scout cookies are sold.
"Shouldn't your drum be metal?"
one girl asks. Not in this sun.
You sing above the rush of traffic
that swishes by in schools. This street
could be filled with muddy water,
as it is months later in the flood,
but today the glint of the sun
hits our eyes, and the sky shines
white above us with only a hint
of turquoise blue, beckoning
blue, afternoon blues blue.
A frog in your throat, you work the crowd
with a gravelly voice, stopping
women on the sidewalk, some
with strollers, who stare.
You charm the crowd with the voodoo
verses of "Hoochie Coochie Man,"
including a black cat bone
and John the Conqueror.
On the sidewalk, in the shade,
as the song says, the pretty women

jump and shout, however now
clicking pictures as you sing,
"You got a boy-child comin',
Gonna be a son-of-a-gun,"
the call of the bluesman,
advertising his own birth.

4. Big Bad Love

Following Elizabeth's Lead

I went into the liquor store first,
and Elizabeth followed, knowing.
It was her idea, and I followed
the sugar in her blood that afternoon.
We got a bottle of Jack
and went across the park,
where we drank in the shadows
of the city trees. Her orange, wavy hair
framed her face like a marigold mane,
and I slipped my hand to her waist,
and we kissed, our bodies moving closer
together near a tree trunk. She loved
to walk barefoot over the sidewalks,
and she walked me to her home,
where she closed her door and set
the padlock. "*My* room," she said.
She was old enough. She paid
rent. Her parents were quiet
somewhere downstairs. She had a mattress
on the floor, and blue sheets.
As the night came on, and we drank more,
she took off her clothes, and I
stripped to my underwear. We lay together
under that blue sheet, and in the morning
there were red circles where we had been,
not unlike the blotches one might make
using a cut potato and red paint.

You'll Need Them All One Day

Her things in two brown grocery bags,
Elizabeth arrived at 51ˢᵗ Street coffee shop,
and I met her. She said, "I'm sleeping
in the park tonight," and I said, "No,
come with me," and she said, "Where?"
And so we got a room at the Westport
Holiday Inn, and I made love
for the first time. She said, "They
labeled me hysterical, took the light
bulbs at night so I wouldn't
cut myself. I thought the night
might never end." Don't we all
secretly wish it, that the sun
might not come around again?

"What was it like?" she said.
I said, "Like being in outer space."
"You're lying," she said.
"This isn't your first time."
Then, we showered together.
She drew suds on my chest,
kissed me, and said, with each kiss
a new hair will grow.
"You'll need them all one day."

Elizabeth's Portrait

On Gary's wall
there is a finger painted portrait
of you, naked. Your skin
is orange, and the background
is blue. How did I know
that you, too, had been here?
On Gary's desk, copies
of *Penthouse* and the glossy reproductions
of the paintings of Manet, one
underneath the other. "I love
them all," Gary says, "and I learn
from them both."

I look at Gary's fingers. That
is where it starts, and this
is where it happens.

I dream of Elizabeth,
and she comes to me
as she is
in one of Gary's paintings.
I do not touch her,
but I wish to. I wish to
touch her again.

Setting Up Chairs
for Lisa

You had Joan Jet black hair
and wore a black leather vest
that seemed a little too tight
around your long torso.
But not too tight.

You sat there, across the room
in a gray folding chair, and I watched you
as Bob Stewart talked. From the podium,
he would adjust his glasses and look across
at us all, and I wondered what he was looking for
and what he saw. He told us
we should volunteer, here
at The Writers Place, in a building
that had been a brothel, a church,
and some lucky someone's elaborate house.
Upstairs, a claw-foot tub sat three.

It was summer, and I was a few minutes
late, driving into the city, and I had rushed
in through the door. I remember sweat
dripping down my cheek.

A few weeks later, I was working
for The Writers Place, and one night,
while setting up the folding chairs,
I thought of you in that black leather outfit,

and dreaming of sitting next to you,
I set up the chairs in narrow rows.

Lisa's Flying Electric Piano

Her full-sized electric piano flew out
of my father's pickup truck.
I was driving. Somehow, the base
detached from the keyboard,
and it all went flying into the busy
intersection of 47th and Main.
No one hit it, and Lisa said,
"Let's just throw it into this
dumpster," when we had carried it
out of the road. "No," I said.
"Let's take it to your new apartment,"
and we did. When I turned it on,
the power eye glowed red,
but it did not play. The next day,
I found the volume slider,
turned it up, and it played perfectly.
Aside from the scrapes from the road
on its key cover, it was fine.
I practiced tying knots, roping things down,
and I dreamt, at last, of turning corners
slow, and of a keyboard
rising in flight and floating across town,
playing a well-known sonata.

Private Yoga Lessons

On the walls were color diagrams
of the spirit. You lived in the pink house then.
It was big and old, and I once tried to anchor
a hook from the ceiling, but only plaster came down
in sprinkles and in chunks. Some evenings,
we would sit in the center of the room, cross-legged
on hardwood floor, and meditate in the approaching darkness,
candles lit on the end tables, incense wafting in
on spirit trails. Your eyes were open. Mine were
closed. I imagined that if I were to look at you
I might turn to stone, or butter, and so I kept
them closed, and I let you lead my body
upward and outward, arms stretching toward
the windows and the walls, feet holding to the floor
as if each foot were an anvil weight, toes spread,
fingertips reaching, pulling the muscles like ropes
on pulleys, stretching both heavenward and earthward.
I did not question. I did not think. I waited
into the weightlessness, and for the star I saw
in my mind to move from left to center.
I can remember the day of my return
to you, how one leg became stiff and leaden
as I walked, as if cursed, wooden like a peg leg,
trying to convince me not to return to your couch,
where I would speak of my dreams and my visions,
and we would wait for evening to come, light to fall,
and for the sound of the crickets, which sometimes, strangely,
spoke in our own tongue.

5. Without a Map

To Eat Just Once:
Remembering a Ranger Lecture at
Yellowstone National Park

For Mel

After they kill, the wolves eat just once.

The pack, all tooth and jaw, with ribcages that jut
like opened Texas toothpick knives, feasts.

Their gray bellies fill and sag with new meat.

They used to eat twice or even three times
from downed prey, a straggling old deer or a slow fawn—

their dead eyes, like tumbled obsidian, still catching light—
the body dragged into an old tree

or quickly buried and left for later.
However, ranchers started poisoning

hidden carcasses so that at the second
meal, the wolves, bloated with pain,

would die. Some, however, did live
and taught the others to eat just once

and leave like a swift wind,
a scattered gray line galloping into night.

After Stephen Hawking's Address on Yahoo!

I hear it takes a star's explosion
to make gold. That much heat
is needed. We too are other-worldly.
There must also be stardust in us.

There must be a reason
we are given a view
of our small part of the universe
12 of every 24 hours—
time to gaze up into the darkness
and spot stars
and muse upon the white face
of the moon in its many phases.

Look past the headlights
and the street lamps with their alien curves
that look like the death-ray guns
of the ships in *War of the Worlds* and wonder:
When will my descendants travel more deeply
into the satin fabric of your black skies?
Where will we go? How will we live,
once we leave this tired, beaten world behind?

Yellowstone Sketches

Everywhere insects weaving
a windless evening.

The water's surface
still as a plateau of drifting ice.

I dare not skip a rock.

Oedipa Discovers the Circuitry of Real Estate: A Montage on Pynchon's *The Crying of Lot 49*

She opens the back of the transistor radio
to replace a battery, and Oedipa Maas
discovers a world of circuitry,
a green circuit board with skyscrapers
dotting its fields, buildings springing up
like new wheat; real estate
crosses her mind, and Inverarity,
her former lover who speculated in land,
leaving her executor of a fortune,
marches across the circuit board in miniature,
a despot, a dictator with shiny black shoes
and dark slacks and a stride that too much
resembles a goose-step, and so Oedipa
closes the battery hatch, turning the radio on
to the voice of her husband, the disk jockey, Mucho
who used to sell used cars and dreams
of sawdust circulating in the engine,
making a cream puff run—
cream puff, a word he can no longer stand
at cocktail parties, his past rushing again
into his present, his voice growing deeper now,
more ominous, more sexy for the 17 year olds.
Mucho Maas is ready to go on the air.

Another Romantic Rendezvous

Always, there is travel involved—
a trip to Paris or New York,
a journey to the top of a tower
that overlooks the rest of us sleeping,
a rendezvous up where the air
is thin. That is where
you two meet, two who would be
lovers once more, be you
Cary Grant and Deborah Kerr,
in *An Affair to Remember*,
or Harry running through the winter night
arriving, again, at the party
desperate now again for Sally,
his heart a hot coal
sizzling in the rain.

This is the way of us,
risking the congregation of martini stares,
of the quiet laugh
coming from the corner—
risking the let down
before the crowd, the loss,
the return through the rain,
the flush of color
gone from your face,
the tears forming
at the corners of your eyes—

but instead she chooses you,
and you return together,
your hand in her hand,
forgetting Sartre's example of bad faith:
her hand taking your hand with indifference.
You move back to where you started,
before this night, when you walked
in a park where the leaves bloomed yellow
and orange with that last breath of autumn.

It was as if the branches held fire.
You walked through it, and you joked,
and you considered holding hands
for that first time, as the forest burned,
flush with color, around you.

6. Chalk on the Walk

Grade School Blacktop Football

We threw long passes, the shadow
of the ball sailing over the blacktop
like a miniature blimp. Our hands
up like weeds up from cracks
in blacktop, all reaching for the same
light, same sun, same golden ball,
just out of reach, the tips of our fingers
touching. Afterward, we sat in a circle
while the teacher read *Where
the Red Fern Grows*, and we toyed
with the flaps of denim
over our knees, where the blood
ran from our game, and sometimes
we went, sand in our knees,
to the nurse, who wiped us with
antiseptic, and we watched
the peroxide bubble.

Coach's Words

"Don't dive deep.
Skip like a thrown stone."
These are words coach uses
to describe how to dive
off the blocks and across
the surface. I hit my head
on the bottom three times,
and coach pulled me from the water
and took me over to the deep end
to try again. "Belly flop first,"
he would say. "That is the feeling.
Now duck your head. Now look up."
I swivel through the water
like a dolphin. I have it now.
I grip my toes around the lip
of the diving block. I kick off
and skip, just like a rock.

Afternoon with Crows

I.
Communion was set
outside on one long dinner table
at the trailer park
retirement center
in Apache Junction, AZ.

II.
I had met a girl
by the pool
and knew her name.

III.
My grandparents
said that there was
no more reason for church.
Card games and yarns
told their stories
better than bible verses,
and too many friends
had already passed
for them to enjoy the service.

IV.
We walked by
the communion table,
and starlings descended.
They took the bread
and toppled and drank
the grape juice and wine
poured into ordinary
little plastic cups.

On My Chalk

My knees were starting to ache
a little, a slight sweet pain,
as I was finishing
the edges of my square—
chalk spread
around my drawing, chalk
half spent or more
than half spent; in
my hand I held a stub
of cerulean blue, chalking in
the sky, when this suit
stops, his shined shoes
in the middle of the clouds
of my drawing, and he looks
down at me and smiles,
like he wants
to pick me up—and
I hold up a piece
of chalk, a white
one. "You can
chalk the clouds back
in now," I say,
and he stops, and he stoops,
and he takes the chalk,
and in that moment
we both wonder
just what he
will do now.

Dear Dad,

You taught me
to lift things, to shoot things.
You taught me every game I know.
I owe you, I give you
every swished basket, every smoked bluerock,
every moved sofa.
Your blood in my muscles,
your grip in my fingers,
along my thumb,
and in the center of my palm—
muscle made for moving,
muscle made for gripping, for holding,
muscle made for balancing a ball
so that every part of the hand takes hold—
how we take hold
when we shake.

Chalk on the Walk

"A zero and a one. Ten," Eliot says, drawing
with chalk on the sidewalk, after watering the flowers.
He traces letters, numbers, and musical notes.
He used to say, "No chalk, Papa,"
but now he allows it.

Drawing this way is primitive,
as if we are some of the first people, drawing
pictures and making signs, creating thought.
Somewhere I read—I think it was Aeschylus
—that "memory is the mother of thought."

Here are glimpses of our memories,
our days and nights, out front
on the walk: a rainbow-colored lizard, an 8,
a bird, a sun, a quarter note, a spider, a web.

Lightning's Bite

Watch out. The lightning might come down
and bite you, my son says, and we look
to the gray, weighted clouds above us
that look like they are carrying heavy sacks
of hail or rain. Or snow, but it is too early for that.
So, we hold out our hands, and look for the droplets
that should come, and there are none.
So, we look to the trees that wave and bend
and to the branches full of big green leaves,
branches that look like the necks of great dragons
twisting and fighting, when all this really is
is wind, and we go home, go inside, and watch
as the lights go out, and we listen to the storm above us.
It is like standing under a bridge as a train goes over.
But this train keeps coming, and rumbling, and my son
puts his hands over his ears. I take him in my arms,
and we do not tremble. We laugh.

Wagon, Lightning

"Because the lightning
might come down
and bite us,"
I pull the red wagon faster,
up hill, on the sidewalk,
past the golf course,
down the red brick street
to our house, stow
the wagon in the garage,
and bring little e. inside,
where we sink into the couch
and watch the lights flash above,
through a darkened window.
As in a cave, we watch
and flip on lights only later,
after we have seen the show
and heard the thunder come rumble
and the smell of rain coming in with the a/c,
putting us swiftly to sleep.

7. Between Rains

Economics of Summer Rain

Summer of yellow scorched leaves
and sand coming up
between dry grass blades.

The tomatoes, something
to constantly water evenings,
giving each clump
a long cool drink
from the winding green
garden hose.

And then it comes,
rain in nickel-sized drops—
spare change everywhere.

Ballet Slippers

slap and knuckle the floor, when up close,
a wooden block tapping through the shoe,
wood meeting wood at the floor's bowed surface—
slatted floors flooded with sunlight,
light caught and held by mirrors—
and dust, dust everywhere. White powder
from the shoes and dust brought to the surface
by feet rising and striking, landing as an insect
does on a long slender leaf,
lifting into flight.

No Saint

Steve was a
pretty good guy, but
he didn't think himself
a saint. This is why
he found it so strange one day
when (after taking
an antidepressant)
he found that his head
began to glow.
It emanated from his
pillow. He kept
his wife up at first.
Then, he slept downstairs
on the couch near the can,
like a night light.

In photographs, Steve's face
was overexposed, as if
his face were a light bulb,
a blast of light atop his shoulders,
as in the Duane Michals photograph
"The Illuminated Man," the spirit
leaving the body through
the bright crown of the head.

In churches, the stained
glass came as an odd omen.
Here were other men
and women
who glowed,
and when they spoke,
they were followed.

Steve took to always wearing a hat.
But at night, when he put
his hat on its hook, he still wondered:
"But what about that glow?"

Banjoman

plays the strings and drums his fingers
in between verses of Cobain's
tune. "Hello, how low, halo," he sings.
On his forehead are deep lines.
His skin is dark, American Indian.
He is about 40, and he wears thick glasses
with even thicker black rims, and I stop
and put a dollar in his case
and just sit there, on a ledge, listening.
He is good. Not all
of the street musicians in Lawrence are.
My wife stands, a distance away,
by a storefront window, and puts her hands
deep into her winter coat pockets, and that
is when it happens, a blonde buzz-cut man
in Eddie Bauer hand-me-downs yells
at our street musician: "You'd better stop
telling lies about me." He thumps
the banjo man on the back. He pulls
a six-inch Case pocketknife.
Banjoman says, "I haven't said
nothin' about you. Are you gonna
stick me with that thing, or aren't you?"
Blondeguy says nothing. Then,
"If I need to." "I've had it
with your aggression, man," says
Banjoman. "Take your violence somewhere
else." And, by now, I've circled them,
come between my wife and the blade,
and motioned for her to follow me
a ways away, to the coffee shop patio,
to the wrought iron tables and chairs.

That One-Legged Man

A semi turns, almost jack-knifing;
it blocks the intersection, and a man
with one leg throws open
his car door and begins hopping
fast, around the truck, and across
traffic. He's wearing burgundy
starter pants and jacket, a black man
in one expensive sneaker—and he's hopping
faster than I've ever seen one man hop,
and people are watching. That's when
the cops start coming—on foot
and on motorcycle—about 8-10 white cops,
guns in the air, running; and our man is hopping
for his life, until they grab him, pull him down,
in one big huddle to the ground, and cuff him,
and it all seems to stop—somewhere
in San Francisco, on the street near
the public library—I see a mob of cops
take down a one-legged man.

Lighting the Ice Storm

Outside, the limbs
are like Laura's glass figurines.
Touch them, and they break.
Even a child's touch
can bring a branch down.
It keeps raining,
and I keep looking at the lamp
above me, and at the computer
screen, for that flicker that means
the power's going out, the cold's
setting in, and we will use
flashlights and candles
to light our way.

Between Rains

the leaves hang down
like a string of green and yellow flags
abandoned when the model home
is sold, but the neighborhood
has not yet sprung up. Everywhere
flowers have dried on their stems,
drooping. Their petals
face the ground, necks bent
and distorted, like men in Klimt
paintings, pulling unnatural angles
with their necks for a kiss.
The flowers drop, when I water them.
Their petals hold the earth,
like fingers grasping sand,
holding to the fringe of the sea,
as in after an accident
in the water. Some small
distance in, our fingers catch,
and we trust the sea, and we do not expect
that shower that then might come,
rain falling, pushing us deeper
toward the earth, reminding us
of our origins in that skim of plankton,
riding the crests and waves—and sea foam,
carrying us along, sending us
into clumps. We look up,
see the sun,
and religion is born.

About the Author:

Kevin Rabas co-directs the Creative Writing Program at Emporia State University, is co-editor of *Flint Hills Review*, and writes regularly for *Jazz Ambassador Magazine (JAM)*. His poems and stories have appeared in *The Malahat Review, Nimrod, Event, The Mid-America Poetry Review,* and elsewhere. He is the winner of the Langston Hughes Award for Poetry and a Salina New Voice Award. Rabas' poems have been nominated for the Pushcart Prize. His first book, *Bird's Horn & Other Poems*, was published by Coal City Review Press. This is his second book.

www.ingramcontent.com/pod-product-compliance
Lightning Source LLC
Chambersburg PA
CBHW061046050726
47592CB00004B/1608